Contents

People in the story

David
is seventeen. He lives in
Hampstead, London,
with his cat.

Ella
is sixteen and she
lives on the street.

Steve
sells drugs.

Socrates
is David's cat.

Starter Level

Series editor: Philip Prowse

03|3   **2 2 MAR 2013**

Book Boy

Antoinette Moses

CAMBRIDGE
UNIVERSITY PRESS

CAMBRIDGE UNIVERSITY PRESS
Cambridge, New York, Melbourne, Madrid, Cape Town, Singapore,
São Paulo, Delhi, Dubai, Tokyo

Cambridge University Press
The Edinburgh Building, Cambridge CB2 8RU, UK

www.cambridge.org
Information on this title: www.cambridge.org/9780521156776

First published 2010

Antoinette Moses has asserted her right to be identified as the Author of the Work in
accordance with the Copyright, Designs and Patents Act 1988.

Printed in China by Sheck Wah Tong Printing Press Limited

Typeset by Aptara Inc.
Illustrations by Nick Hardcastle
Map artwork by Malcolm Barnes

A catalogue record for this publication is available from the British Library.

ISBN 978-0-521-15677-6 paperback
ISBN 978-0-521-18270-6 paperback plus audio CD

Places in the story

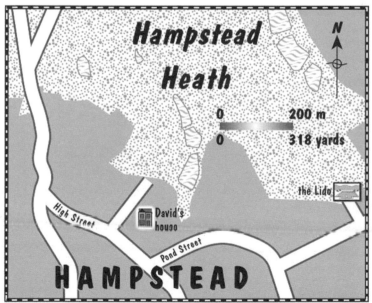

Chapter 1 *Books are my life*

My name is David and this is my room. There are lots of books in the room. And a cat. His name is Socrates. Why? Because he thinks all day.

No. Again.

This is a book about books. My name is David and books are my life. There are so many worlds in books. In books, I can be anybody. Books are my friends.

Friends? No. That's not good. Books are my world? Again.

This is my house.

Well, no, it isn't. It's my mother and father's house, but they're dead.

So, it's my house, but nobody knows that. Everybody here thinks that my parents are in Canada. My aunt knows that they're dead, but she's not here. She lives in Canada.

My aunt thinks I'm at a friend's house. She thinks there's no-one in this house. She gives me money. It's not a lot, but I can buy food for Socrates and pizza for me. My aunt is going to come here in September. Now it's June.

But all this isn't important. In a book you need a story.

David Sims is seventeen. His mother and father are dead. He lives in Hampstead with his cat, Socrates, and three thousand books.

Is it three thousand? I don't know. Four thousand? This is stupid. I'm going to start again.

My name is David and I'm writing a book about my life.

No. This is wrong. I don't have a life. My life is: I read books and I talk to my cat. And I eat pizza every day and … and … my life is books. No, that's really stupid. I want to write a book. But I need a story and I don't have a story. I'm going to start again. No, I'm going to get a pizza and then I'm going to find a story.

'Is that OK?' I ask Socrates.

Socrates says, 'I want fish.'

No, he doesn't. He's a cat; he can't talk. But he says, 'Miaow' and 'Miaow' is 'I want food.' 'Miaow' is also 'I want your bed.'

'OK,' I say to Socrates. 'I'm going to get some cat food. Then I'm going to get my pizza.'

I like pizza. I eat it every day.

I buy the cat food and then I go to a bookshop. They have lots of old books and sometimes I buy one. Then I go to a café in the High Street.

Today I see a girl outside the café. I think she's sleeping. I walk into the café. I'm hungry and I want a pizza.

Chapter 2   *Ella*

When I come out with my pizza I see the girl again. She isn't sleeping now. She looks cold and hungry. I stop.

'Hello,' I say.

'Have you got a pound?' the girl asks.

'Yes,' I say. 'Are you hungry? I've got a pizza. Do you like pizza?'

'I don't eat anchovies,' says the girl.

'Anchovies?' I say.

'Small fish, lots of salt,' she says.

'I know what anchovies are. There aren't any anchovies on this pizza.' I laugh. 'Socrates likes anchovies, but I don't.'

'Socrates?' she asks. I think she's about sixteen, and she's pretty, but very thin.

'Socrates is my cat,' I say. 'And I'm David,' I tell her.

'My name's Ella,' says the girl. 'Now, where's this pizza?'

The pizza is good. We eat and don't talk. Then Ella smiles.

'Are you a student?' she asks.

'No,' I say. 'But I'm going to be a student. In October.'

'But you're not at school,' she says.

'No,' I say. 'I don't go to school now. I'm seventeen.'

'Do you live with your mother and father?' she asks.

'You ask a lot of questions,' I say. 'No, I don't. My mother and father are dead.'

'My father's in prison,' says Ella.

'Oh,' I say. 'Why?'

'I don't talk about it,' Ella answers.

'I'm sorry,' I say. I look at Ella. It's a hot day, but she looks cold.

'Are you OK?' I ask. 'Are you cold?'

'I'm always cold,' Ella answers. 'I'm cold because I'm tired.'

'My house is near here,' I say. 'You can come back with me. And you can meet Socrates.'

* * *

'Wow! You must have a million books,' says Ella.

'Yes,' I say. I want to ask Ella a lot of questions, but I don't know where to start.

'Can I have a bath?' asks Ella.

'Of course,' I say. I look at Ella. Her clothes are really dirty. My mother's clothes are still in the house. But they aren't her clothes now, because she's dead. No. I can't think about that. But my mother's clothes are clean and Ella needs clean clothes.

I go into my parents' room and find some clothes for Ella. I don't often go into this room. My parents' things are all still here. I don't want to think about my mother and father. But I think about them every day. I don't want them to be dead. I want them here, with me.

Ella looks good after her bath. She's wearing my mother's dress.

She tells me something about her life. She comes from Leeds. That's where her mother lives. Her mother drinks a lot. Ella doesn't like her mother. I think she's bad to Ella. Ella has a friend in London called Steve. I think he's a friend, but I also think she's afraid of him.

I tell Ella about my parents, and my aunt in Canada.

'So you live here now with your cat?' she asks.

'Yes,' I answer.

'It's a very big house for one person,' she says.

'Do you want to live here?' I ask. I don't know why I say this.

'You're a nice boy,' says Ella. 'But you don't know anything about me. You don't know me. I'm not a good person.'

'I like you,' I say. 'It's OK.'

'You don't understand,' says Ella. 'You live in a house. I live on the street. The street is bad.'

Chapter 3   *Where's my laptop?*

'You don't understand the street,' says Ella.

'Tell me,' I say. 'I'm listening.'

'OK,' says Ella. 'Everybody walks down the street, but they don't live there. They see me and they walk on.'

'I stopped,' I say.

'You're not everybody,' says Ella. 'People walk on and people go home. But on the street there's no home. There's only the street, and it's England and it's cold. It's always cold on the street. And you can't sleep.'

I look at Ella and I think about her words. I'm not a rich person. I don't have a lot of money, but I have a home.

'On the street, you sleep for an hour or two hours on a good night,' says Ella. 'But you're always afraid. People come and kick you.'

'That's my world,' says Ella. 'Think about it. You're always tired and you're always cold. The cold gets inside you.'

I'm beginning to understand. Ella is telling me something about herself, about her world. On the street you need something to help you.

'Drink?' I ask. 'Drugs?'

I look at Ella and I understand.

'That's life on the street, Ella,' I say. 'You can live in my house, but I don't want drugs here. I don't like drugs.'

'That's OK. I don't need drugs here,' says Ella. 'I'm not cold here and I'm not afraid. And I can sleep.'

* * *

I like Ella. She tells me about her world and I write the stories on my laptop. She cooks sometimes and she sings. I feel happy with Ella in the house.

Socrates likes Ella too. Days go by. One week. Two weeks. Then something changes. I don't know what it is, but Ella isn't singing. She doesn't want to cook. She talks to people on the phone. I can't hear what she says. I don't think she's happy.

* * *

It's a hot day and I want to go swimming.

'It's hot today,' I say to Ella. 'There's a swimming pool near here – the Lido. We can go swimming there. It's good.'

'I can't swim,' Ella says. 'I like this house. I don't want to go out.'

'OK,' I say. 'You can talk to Socrates.'

'We need milk and eggs,' says Ella.

'OK,' I say. 'I can get them at the shop.'

There are lots of people at the pool. It's good there. I love the Lido. I come home at about seven.

'Hi, Ella!' I shout. 'I'm home. I've got the eggs and milk and I've got ice cream! Ella? Ella!'

Ella isn't here. And where's my laptop?

Chapter 4 *I don't need Ella*

Socrates and I don't need Ella. We're OK without her. I don't think about Ella. I don't think about Ella's cooking. I don't think about Ella with Socrates. I swim and I read. I'm OK.

No, I'm not. I want Ella and I want my laptop. It's got all my stories about Ella.

And now I think about Ella on the street again. Is she hungry? Is she afraid?

'I'm going to find Ella,' I tell Socrates. 'She's only sixteen. She needs a home.' And a friend, I think. She needs me.

They say there are 7,560,000 people in London. That's a lot of people. And Ella's just one girl in a very big city. Where is she?

I can't go to the police. Ella doesn't like them. The police mustn't find her.

'Where's Ella?' I ask Socrates.

'Miaow,' he says. Food.

Cats can't find people. Cats can't do anything.

'I need a dog,' I tell Socrates. He looks at me, and I feel bad. 'I'm sorry,' I say. 'I don't need a dog.'

I think about Ella and life on the street. 'You don't go far,' she says. So I start with Hampstead High Street. Ella knows the High Street. I have a picture of Ella on my phone. I take it with me into the shops.

'Do you know this girl?' I ask.

'No,' say the people in the first shop. I go into all the shops in the High Street. Everyone says no.

21

I'm tired. Nobody knows Ella. But in the afternoon I ask an old man in the street. He knows Ella.

'There's an old house in Pond Street,' he tells me. 'No-one lives there. But I see lights at night. There are people there sometimes.'

I go there. It's a big house. The door is open, and I go in. It's very dirty and it's dark. I can't see anything, but I hear a noise. 'Hello!' I shout.

'David?' somebody answers. It's Ella!
'Ella!' I say.
'I'm sorry,' says Ella.
'It's OK,' I say. 'I'm here.'
'I want to go home,' says Ella. 'I want Socrates.'

Chapter 5 *Steve*

Ella comes home with me. She sleeps for two days. Socrates sits by the bed and watches her. Then she gets up and has a bath. She looks OK now, but her face is still blue and yellow.

'I must go now,' says Ella.

'No,' I say. 'You can live here.'

'No, I can't,' says Ella. 'Steve's going to come here again.'

'Again?' I ask.

'Steve has your laptop,' she answers.

'I'm not afraid of Steve,' I tell her.

'Then you're stupid,' says Ella. 'Steve's bad, very bad. David, listen to me. Steve's got a gun.'

A gun? This isn't my life. I don't live in a world with guns. In books people have guns. In films people have guns. I know there are guns in London, but not here in Hampstead. People don't have guns here.

'Ella, we must go to the police,' I say. 'You must tell them about Steve.'

'Oh, David,' says Ella. 'You still don't understand anything. I need drugs.'

'You don't need drugs,' I tell her.

'I try,' says Ella. 'I come here. I think I don't need drugs. But it's not easy.'

'You can stop,' I say, but I'm just saying words. It's not easy to stop taking drugs.

'I don't like Steve, but he gives me drugs. I sell drugs for him.'

I don't know what to say.

Ella is talking to Socrates.

'You're a good cat,' she says. 'You must tell David that pizza every day isn't good.' And Ella starts to cry.

'Miaow,' says Socrates.

'Yes, David needs food.' Now Ella is laughing and crying. Then we hear a noise outside the house and she stops laughing.

'Oh no,' says Ella. 'It's Steve!'

Steve comes in. He doesn't say hello.

'Ella,' says Steve. 'What are you doing here?'

'Ella lives here,' I say.

'No,' says Steve. 'Ella lives with me. Ella works for me.'

I'm afraid, but I don't want Steve to know this.

'Ella's my friend and she isn't going anywhere,' I say. 'I can phone the police.'

Steve laughs. 'Ella!' he shouts. 'Come here!'

'Ella's my friend,' I say again. 'She's not going with you.'

'No?' Steve says. 'Are you going to stop me?'

'Yes,' I say.

'What are you going to do?' Steve laughs. 'Are you going to read to me, book boy?'

Steve comes over to me and I can't do anything. I'm not a person from a book; I don't know what to do. I'm really afraid.

Chapter 6 *A new life*

Everything goes very fast. Steve comes over to me, but Socrates is there and Steve stands on him. Socrates is angry, and says 'Miaow!' very loudly. Steve kicks Socrates, and Socrates jumps on to his face.

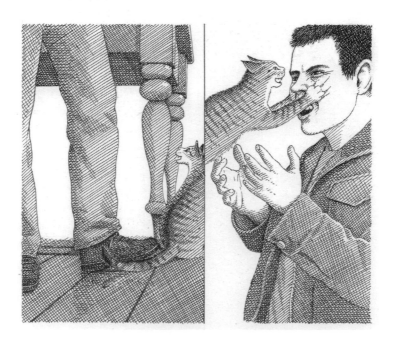

'Ow!' Steve shouts. Socrates doesn't like Steve and he's very angry now. Steve isn't watching Ella and me. Socrates is on his face. Ella picks up a big book and hits Steve on the head.

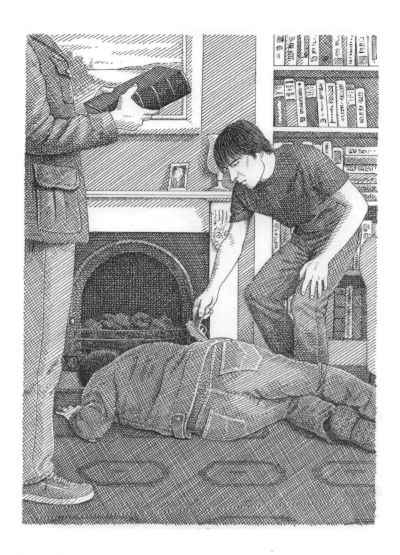

I take the gun.

'Is he dead?' Ella asks.

I look at Steve. He makes a small noise. 'No,' I answer. 'Steve isn't dead, but I'm watching him. You phone the police.'

The police come and we all go to the police station.

* * *

In a book that's the end of the story. The police come and the bad person goes to prison.

But this is my story and my life is starting again. And it's good.

My aunt comes over from Canada. She likes Ella. My aunt phones an organisation called Centrepoint. Centrepoint helps young people who live on the street. The people at Centrepoint talk to Ella's mother and she talks to my aunt. And everybody says that Ella can live here with my aunt and me. And now Ella isn't afraid, because Steve is in prison. The police say he's going to be in prison for a long time.

The story about Steve and Socrates is in the newspapers. Socrates is famous. Everybody wants to know about him. They ask me, 'What does Socrates eat? Where does Socrates sleep?'

* * *

I'm eighteen now and Ella is seventeen. Ella and I are happy.

Ella works at Centrepoint. She helps other young people on the street. And she goes to schools and talks about drugs. Students listen to Ella because she knows life on the street.

And I write stories. This is one story and it isn't about books. It's about me and Ella. Now I know that you need people in stories. And you need people in your life. I'm not a book boy now. I have good friends and a famous cat!